TEEN TITANS GO!

IDOL HANDS AND COLD BLOODED

Raintree is an imprint of Capstone Global Library Limited, a company incorporated in England and Wales having its
registered office at 264 Banbury Road, Oxford, OX2 7DY – Registered company number: 6695582

www.raintree.co.uk
myorders@raintree.co.uk

Edited by Chris Harbo
Designed by Brann Garvey and Hilary Wacholz
Production by Kathy McColley
Originated by Capstone Global Library Ltd
Printed and bound in India

ISBN 978 1 4747 7323 2
22 21 20 19
10 9 8 7 6 5 4 3 2

British Library Cataloguing in Publication Data
A full catalogue record for this book is available from the British Library

TEEN TITANS GO!™

SHOLLY FISCH MERRILL HAGAN
WRITERS

LEA HERNANDEZ JORGE CORONA
ARTISTS

JEREMY LAWSON
COLOURIST

WES ABBOTT
LETTERER

DAN HIPP
COVER ARTIST

raintree
a Capstone company — publishers for children

EEEEEK!

AAGH! ALLIGATOR!

INCOMING!

SPLURRRCH

KA-BOOOM

MONSTER MOVIE?

NOPE--

DURRN DUKKIT

--REALITY SHOW.

... AND THAT WAS **THE ARISTOCRATS!**

WE'LL SEE HOW OUR CELEBRITY JUDGES RATED THEIR ACT WHEN WE RETURN TO **JUMP CITY'S GOT YOUR TALENT** RIGHT HERE! WE'LL BE BACK IN A MOMENT--

--RIGHT AFTER WE PUT OUT THE **FIRE!**

THIS IS THE AWESOMEST SHOW **EVER!**

I MEAN, WHERE ELSE CAN YOU SEE A DANCING BEAR **JUGGLING** A TRIO OF **ONE-ARMED PIANISTS?**

I KNOW, RIGHT? BUT THE **BEST** PART IS WHEN THE **JUDGES** RIP INTO THE TALENTLESS **LOSERS!**

OH, JOY. PUBLIC HUMILIATION.

WOO-HOO.

MY FRIENDS, I AM MOST *PLEASED* TO WITNESS THE ENJOYMENT YOU ALL DERIVE FROM THE *TELEVISED REALITY*--

--FOR I HAVE *SIGNED* US UP TO COMPETE ON *NEXT WEEK'S* BROADCAST!

"IDOL HANDS"

WRITTEN BY **SHOLLY FISCH** ART BY **LEA HERNANDEZ** LETTERS BY **WES ABBOTT** COVER BY **DAN HIPP** EDITED BY **ALEX ANTONE**

NO!

YES!

YOU *CAN'T* BE SERIOUS, STARFIRE! WHY WOULD ANYONE VOLUNTEER TO HAVE THEIR SELF-ESTEEM *TORN TO SHREDS* LIKE THAT? WHY WOULD WE WANT TO ENDURE *RIDICULE* IN FRONT OF TWENTY MILLION PEOPLE?

DUHH! TO BE ON *TV!*

OH, YEAH!

I GOT MOVES LIKE *JAGUAR,* BABY!

I KNOW WHAT WE CAN DO! WATCH ME SPIN THIS *PLATE* ON A *STICK!*

SMASSH

OOPS.

YOU HAVE TO CALL THEM BACK AND *CANCEL* BEFORE EVERYONE GETS *COMPLETELY* CARRIED AWAY!

BUT IS THAT NOT THE *POINT?* TO BE *CARRIED AWAY* ON *WINGS OF WHIMSY?*

OKAY, MAYBE *THIS* PLATE.

SMASSH

OR *THIS* ONE.

SMASSH

OR *THIS* ONE.

SMASSH

ROBIN! BE THE VOICE OF *SANITY* HERE!

RIGHT! I'M THE LEADER OF THE TITANS, AND I SAY--

--WE ARE ABSOLUTELY *NOT* DOING THIS!

PRETTY PLEASE

BUT, ROBIN...

...Pretty please?

AH... GAH... GOO...

RIGHT! I'M THE LEADER OF THE TITANS, AND I SAY--

--WE ARE ABSOLUTELY *DOING* THIS!

THAT MEANS WE NEED *TRAINING!* CALISTHENICS AT *FIVE A.M.* EVERY DAY, FOLLOWED BY ROUND-THE-CLOCK *REHEARSALS*, *TAP DANCING*, AND *CELEBRITY TANNING!*

FIVE A.M... IN THE *MORNING?*

UM, I DON'T REALLY *TAN*...

NO TIME FOR CHIT CHAT! *GO, GO, GO!*

WE'VE ONLY GOT *ONE WEEK*--

JUMP CITY'S GOT YOUR TALENT RIGHT HERE!

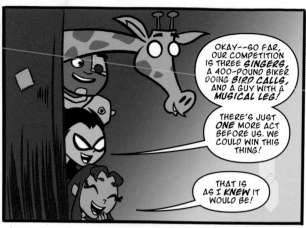

WELCOME BACK! IT'S *SHOWTIME!*

THERE ARE ONLY *TWO* MORE ACTS TO GO, SO LET'S MEET THE FIRST RIGHT NOW...

OKAY--SO FAR, OUR COMPETITION IS THREE *SINGERS*, A 400-POUND BIKER DOING *BIRD CALLS*, AND A GUY WITH A *MUSICAL LEG!*

THERE'S JUST *ONE* MORE ACT BEFORE US. WE COULD WIN THIS THING!

THAT IS AS I *KNEW* IT WOULD BE!

OUR UNIQUE TALENTS ARE NOT EASILY SURPASSED. MOST ACTS CANNOT *FLY* OR *TURN INTO ANIMALS!*

AN ANIMAL ACT. THAT'S ALMOST AS CUTTING-EDGE AS A MIME.

MIME! WHAT AN *EXCELLENT* IDEA, RAVEN!

YOU COULD PERFORM CLASSIC EXAMPLES OF THE *MIME*--SUCH AS "MAN WALKING INTO THE *GRLZBLAX!*"

OR "MAN POUNDED INTO THE DIRT BY A *TWO-TON SNORZFLOR!*"

ASSUMING THE GRLZBLAX DOES NOT MIND.

KILL ME NOW.

AW, YOU'RE JUST JEALOUS BECAUSE YOUR ONLY TALENT IS SUCKING ALL THE FUN OUT OF A ROOM!

OH, REALLY?

SHH! KEEP IT DOWN! THE NEXT ACT'S COMING OUT!

YIKE!

...AND HERE THEY ARE NOW! PLEASE WELCOME--

CRUNCH

--THE BROTHERHOOD OF **EVIL!**

THE BROTHERHOOD--

--OF THE **EVIL?!**

WHY DON'T YOU **INTRODUCE** YOURSELVES TO OUR **AUDIENCE?**

CERTAINMENT! I AM THE **BRAIN.** THIS IS--

--THE CRIMINALLY TWISTED **MADAME ROUGE**--

--THE SIMIAN GENIUS, **MONSIEUR MALLAH**--

--**PHOBIA,** THE MISTRESS OF FEAR--

--AND **PLASMUS,** WHOSE BURNING TOUCH MEANS **DEATH!**

AND WHAT WILL YOU **WACKY** KIDS BE **DOING** FOR US TONIGHT?

I WILL SING AN A CAPELLA MEDLEY OF **LADY GAGA** SONGS, WHILE MY ASSOCIATES PERFORM **INTERPRETIVE DANCE.**

ONE TITANIC, EARTH-SHATTERING BATTLE LATER--

UH-HUH! THAT'S RIGHT!

SO MUCH FOR THE BROTHERHOOD OF--LAME!

HIGH FIVE!

TEEN TITANS RULE!

JUMP CITY'S GOT YOUR TALENT RIGHT HERE!

BONK

AH-AH-AH--NOT SO FAST! DO THE TEEN TITANS RULE?

THAT'S FOR OUR PANEL OF WASHED-UP CELEBRITY JUDGES TO DECIDE!

GOLDEN AGE SUPER-HERO THE RED BEE?

-PFF!- WHAT WAS ALL THAT?! ENERGY BLASTS? A TYRANNOSAURUS? YOU CALL THAT CRIME-FIGHTING?

IN MY DAY, WE KNEW HOW TO FIGHT CRIME-- --WITH TRAINED BEES!

FORMER CHILD STAR OF DATE WITH DEBBI, DEBBI ANDERSON?

WELL, JEEPERS! I THINK IT'S JUST SWELL TO SEE YOUNG PEOPLE FOLLOWING THEIR DREAM! I'D LIKE TO APPLAUD THEIR EFFORT-- --BUT THEIR SKILLS ARE STRICTLY FROM NOWHERESVILLE.

Product Placement

AND, LAST BUT NOT LEAST, WHAT DO YOU SAY-- --DARKSEID?

DREADFUL. SIMPLY DREADFUL.

THE END

WHO'S THIS DUDE? PARKA KING?

IT'S CAPTAIN COLD, AND WE NEED TO GET HIM OUT OF JUMP CITY!

TITANS GO!

"COLD BLOODED"

WRITTEN BY MERRILL HAGAN

ART BY JORGE CORONA

COLOR BY JEREMY LAWSON

LETTERS BY WES ABBOTT

COVER BY DAN HIPP

EDITED BY ALEX ANTONE

I'M NOT READY TO GO JUST QUITE YET, YA LITTLE PUNK!

WHOA.

DUDE. YOU CAN FREEZE PEOPLE SOLID?

UM, I GUESS SO? USUALLY THE FLASH JUST RUNS AROUND MY BLASTS.

HE'S, UH, PRETTY, PRETTY FAST.

WE MUST TAKE DOWN THIS COLD COMMANDER!

UH-OH.

CAPTAIN COLD'S DOWN.

NOW HOW DO WE GET ROBIN OUT OF THIS ICE?

WE COULD JUST TAKE HIM HOME AND PLAY HOCKEY ON TOP OF HIM UNTIL HE MELTS.

HOW WOULD THAT GET HIM OUT?

I DON'T KNOW. I JUST REALLY WANT AN AIR HOCKEY TABLE.

SNOW CONES

WE COULD HAVE A FUND RAISER WHERE WE SELL ROBIN SNOW CONES AND I SHAVE ICE OFF THE BLOCK BIT BY BIT UNTIL ROBIN'S FREE.

I SAY WE JUST DUMP HIM IN THE HARBOR AND LET HIM FLOAT OUT TO SEA. LET AQUALAD FIGURE IT OUT.

WHAT IF WE ALL DRESS UP LIKE WE'RE FROM THE FUTURE AND WHEN ROBIN GETS OUT OF THE ICE, WE MAKE HIM THINK THAT DECADES HAVE PASSED HIM BY WHILE HE WAS TRAPPED?

AMAZING! LET'S DO THAT ONE.

FRIENDS, ROBIN IS FREE FROM THE ICE!

AWWWW, I WANTED TO DO MY PLAN.

HOW ARE YOU FEELING NOW, ROBIN?

I'M NOT SURE. I THINK THE BLOCK MAY HAVE...MAY HAVE...

=AH-CHOOOOO!=

OH, NO! ROBIN, I THINK YOUR TIME IN THE ICE MIGHT HAVE MADE YOU SICK. YOU NEED TO GET SOME REST.

IT'S JUST A LITTLE HEAD COLD. I DON'T NEED TO GET REST.

YES, YOU DO! I CAN'T HAVE YOUR HEAD COLD SPREADING! ALL I HAVE LEFT IS HEAD!

I CAN'T HAVE ALL THAT MUCOUS DRIPPING DOWN INTO MY DELICATE WIRE-Y PARTS! I'LL SHORT OUT!

DUDE! WE'LL CALL YOU SNOT ROCKET!

I'M TOTALLY FINE. I DON'T NEED TO REST!

JUST GET SOME SHUT-EYE, DUDE.

WE NEED YOU BETTER IN CASE SOMETHING HAPPENS IN JUMP CITY.

UH-OH.

I KNEW YOU JINXED US AS SOON AS YOU SAID IT...

AN ALARM!

TITANS... GAH...GAH... AHHHHHH...

:...CHOOOOO!:

TELL ME YOU DIDN'T JUST SNEEZE INTO MY CLOAK!

GO TO YOUR ROOM AND REST!

ROBIN, PLEASE PROMISE ME YOU'LL STAY IN BED UNTIL YOU GET BETTER. WE NEED YOU ON THE TEAM.

ALL RIGHT, STAR.

I PROMISE. I'LL STAY IN BED UNTIL I'M BETTER.

THANK YOU, ROBIN. NOW I MUST REJOIN THE TEAM AND SAVE THE CITY.

SO WHO ARE WE FIGHTING?

IT'S PRETTY BAD OUT THERE, BEAST BOY.

PLASMUS IS STOMPING THE HARBOR, BUT MAMMOTH IS ALSO TRYING TO ROB A BANK IN DOWNTOWN.

WHAT DO WE DO?

I'LL TELL YOU WHAT TO DO.

OH, MAN. YOU PROMISED...

ROBIN, YOU PROMISED TO STAY IN BED!

I AM IN BED! IN FACT...

I'M IN THE **ULTIMATE BATTLE BED.**

THE ULTIMATE BATTLE BED? MORE LIKE THE ONLY BATTLE BED. THIS IS THE DUMBEST THING I'VE EVER SEEN.

HEY, EVIL DOESN'T WAIT FOR A HERO TO FEEL BETTER. SOMETIMES YOU HAVE TO ROLL INTO BATTLE IN A DIFFERENT WAY.

YEAH, WELL, GOOD LUCK ROLLING INTO BATTLE WITH NO TIRES.

HEY!

PINCH

I DON'T WANT TO BE SICK! I JUST WANT TO HELP!

ROBIN...

PLEASE, JUST GET BETTER.

LATER.

THOSE GUYS WEREN'T SO TOUGH.

I WONDER HOW ROBIN IS DOING.

ROBIN? ARE YOU IN HERE?

STARFIRE? IS THAT YOU?

SMART IDEA MAKING ME STAY HOME. I'M ALL BETTER NOW, THANKS TO YOU.

COME HERE AND GIVE ME A HUG.

UM, OKAY. I WILL GIVE YOU THE HUG. I JUST...

...NEED...

PLEASE EXCUSE ME FOR JUST A MOMENT.

WE NEED TO FIND A WAY TO MAKE ROBIN BETTER. AS QUICKLY AS POSSIBLE.

HOW ARE WE GOING TO DO...

I KNOW WHAT TO DO.

OUR ENEMY IS THE COLD VIRUS INSIDE ROBIN. SO IN ORDER TO WIN, WE MUST FIGHT OUR ENEMY ON HIS TERRITORY.

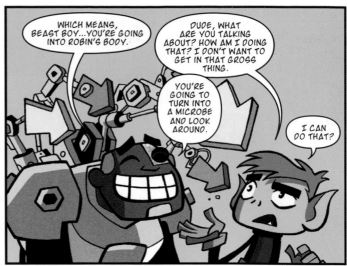

WHICH MEANS, BEAST BOY...YOU'RE GOING INTO ROBIN'S BODY.

DUDE, WHAT ARE YOU TALKING ABOUT? HOW AM I DOING THAT? I DON'T WANT TO GET IN THAT GROSS THING.

YOU'RE GOING TO TURN INTO A MICROBE AND LOOK AROUND.

I CAN DO THAT?

RAVEN, YOU USE THIS TO COMMUNICATE WITH BEAST BOY WHEN HE GETS INSIDE. AND BB, YOU SWALLOW THAT DEVICE SO RAVEN CAN TALK WITH YOU.

STAR, HOW'S IT GOING OVER THERE?

PLEASE, ROBIN. JUST EAT THIS NOODLE OF THE CHICKEN SOUP. IT HAS A SLEEP AGENT SO YOU CAN REST WHILE BEAST BOY FIGHTS THE VIRUS.

I DON'T LIKE THIS PLAN. BEAST BOY MESSES UP ALL OF MY STUFF WHEN HE'S OUTSIDE OF MY BODY. I DON'T EVEN WANT TO KNOW WHAT HE'S GOING TO DO WHEN HE'S INSIDE OF IT.

TRUST ME, PAL, IT'S NOT EXACTLY GOING TO BE A PLEASURE TRIP HIKING THROUGH YOUR INSIDES.

JUST GET IN THERE!

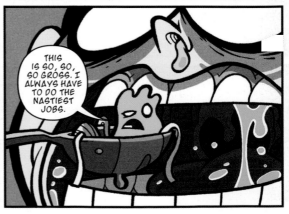

THIS IS SO, SO, SO GROSS. I ALWAYS HAVE TO DO THE NASTIEST JOBS.

NOOOOOOOO!!

TELL BEAST BOY TO HURRY UP. ROBIN'S GETTING SICKER.

GUYS? I THINK I'VE FOUND THE VIRUS!

FIGHT IT, BEAST BOY!

HOW?

ROBIN MAKES US TAKE FIGHT TRAINING EVERY MORNING OF OUR LIVES! USE YOUR SKILLS.

I'M TRYING BUT STUPID MICROBES DON'T HAVE A WHOLE LOT IN THE LIMB DEPARTMENT!

DO SOMETHING! DO ANYTHING!

OKAY...

WAIT! DON'T USE YOUR POWERS INSIDE ROBIN!

CRASH

NOOOOOOOOC!!!

FAINT

DID I GET THE VIRUS?

24

THE END!

CREATORS

SHOLLY FISCH

Bitten by a radioactive typewriter, Sholly Fisch has spent the wee hours writing books, comics, TV scripts and online material for over 25 years. His comic book credits include more than 200 stories and features about characters such as Batman, Superman, Bugs Bunny, Daffy Duck, Spider-Man and Ben 10. Currently, he writes stories for Action Comics every month, plus stories for Looney Tunes and Scooby-Doo. By day, Sholly is a mild-mannered developmental psychologist who helps to create educational TV programmes, websites and other media for kids.

MERRILL HAGAN

Merrill Hagan is a writer who has worked on numerous episodes of the hit *Teen Titans Go!* TV show. In addition, he has written several *Teen Titans Go!* comic books and was a writer for the original *Teen Titans* series in 2003.

LEA HERNANDEZ

Lea Hernandez is a comic book artist and webcomic creator who is known for her manga-influenced style. She has worked with Marvel Comics, Oni Press, NBM Publishing and DC Comics. In addition to her work on *Teen Titans Go!*, she is the co-creator of *Killer Princesses* and the creator of *Rumble Girls*.

JORGE CORONA

Jorge Corona is a Venezuelan comic book artist who is well known for his all-ages fantasy-adventure series *Feathers* and his work on *Jim Henson's The Storyteller: Dragons*. In addition to *Teen Titans Go!*, he has also worked on *Batman Beyond*, *Justice League Beyond*, *We Are Robin*, *Goners* and many other comics.

GLOSSARY

a cappella singing without instrumentation

associate partner or someone you work with

broadcast television or radio programme

calisthenics exercises for improving fitness

condemn force someone to suffer something unpleasant

derive get from something

diabolical extremely wicked

eternal seemingly endless time period

GPS electronic tool used to find the location of an object

humiliation feeling of embarrassment or foolishness

implant put a device into the body by surgery

interpretive dance type of dance that shows emotions or tells a story

jinx bring bad luck

microbe living thing that is too small to see without a microscope

mime performer who expresses himself or herself without words

mucous slimy, thick fluid

paparazzi aggressive photographers who take pictures of celebrities for sale to magazines or newspapers

pun play on words involving the deliberate confusion of similar words or phrases

ridicule harsh criticism or teasing

sanity ability to think and behave in a normal manner

self-esteem feeling of pride and respect for oneself

simian relating to monkeys or apes

surpass be greater or stronger than another person or thing

torment great pain and suffering

virus germ that infects living things and causes diseases

whimsy playful or fanciful behaviour

witness see something happen

VISUAL QUESTIONS & WRITING PROMPTS

1. Why does Robin change his mind about performing on the reality TV show? What clues in these panels support your answer?

2. Why are the Teen Titans drawn differently in this panel? How does the style of the drawings reflect how they are feeling?

3. Make a list of things Robin keeps in his room.
   What sorts of interests and hobbies does he have?
   Discuss how you know.

4. Based on the shape of Robin's arm, what do you think
   Beast Boy turned into? Explain why you think so.

READ THEM ALL!

TEEN TITANS GO!™